RESTING YOUR HEART IN HIM

Confessions to a Loving God

SAINT AUGUSTINE

WHITAKER HOUSE

All Scripture quotations are taken from the King James Version of the Holy Bible.

Publisher's Note: Saint Augustine's language has been slightly updated for the modern reader. Some words, spellings, and sentence structure have been revised for clarity and readability. This book includes selections from the Whitaker House edition of *The Confessions of Saint Augustine*, a revision of the highly respected Edward B. Pusey English translation; *The Meditations of St. Augustine, His Treatise of the Love of God, Soliloquies, and Manual,* translated by George Stanhope in 1701 and printed in London in 1818; *The City of God*, translated by Marcus Dods in 1871; and *King Alfred's Old English Version of St. Augustine's Soliloquies Turned into Modern English* by Henry Lee Hargrove in 1904.

Resting Your Heart in Him
Confessions to a Loving God

ISBN: 979-8-88769-229-6
eBook ISBN: 979-8-88769-230-2
Printed in Colombia

Editor: Peg Fallon

Whitaker House
1030 Hunt Valley Circle
New Kensington, PA 15068
www.whitakerhouse.com

Library of Congress Control Number: 2024937249

1 2 3 4 5 6 7 8 9 10 31 30 29 28 27 26 25 24

ABOUT SAINT AUGUSTINE AND *RESTING YOUR HEART IN HIM*

Aurelius Augustinus (354–430), better known as Saint Augustine, was born to poor parents in the small town of Thagaste in Numidia, North Africa (present-day Algeria). His father, Patricius, a pagan who lived somewhat of a loose life, was converted to Christianity before his death; his mother, Monica, on account of her personal piety and her influence on her son, is one of the most revered women in the history of the Christian church.

Educated at the University of Carthage, Augustine, according to his own account, belonged to a group of rowdy friends and joined in their intemperate living. While there, he entered into a fourteen-year relationship with a young woman who became the mother of his son, Adeodatus. He also joined the heretical sect of the Manicheans, who professed to have received from their founder a higher form of truth than was taught by Christ.

At the close of his university career, which had been brilliant in spite of distractions, he returned to his native town. There, and later in Carthage and Rome, he taught rhetoric, training young lawyers in the art of debating. By the time he was about twenty-seven, Augustine had begun to have doubts as to the validity of the Manichean faith, but it was not until 387, while he was professor at the University of Milan, that he was converted to Christianity and received baptism. He then gave up his profession and became an ascetic, studying the foundations of faith; writing, chiefly against his former sect; and conversing with a group of disciples, first at Rome and then in his native town.

When he was on a visit to Hippo, not far from Thagaste, he went into the priesthood, and in 395, he became bishop of Hippo, an office which he filled for the remaining thirty-five years of his life. Though he took a leading part in the activities of the African church through all this time, and gradually became one of the most distinguished ecclesiastical figures in the Roman Empire, the care of his diocese and the writing of his books formed his chief occupations. He continued to lead a life of extreme simplicity and self-denial, and in his pastoral establishment he trained a large number of disciples who became leaders in the church. The strength of his hold on these younger men was due not merely to his intellectual ascendancy but also to the charm and sweetness of his disposition.

Augustine wrote more than one hundred works that still survive, including the books we have excerpted here, as well as commentaries on Scripture, sermons, and letters.

The Soliloquies provides a penetrating look into Augustine's thought processes right after his conversion to Christianity.

Written in 386–387, it consists of an inner dialogue between himself and his reason, as he poses questions and provides answers while searching for truth, God, and the nature of the soul. This book was translated from Latin into Old English by Anglo-Saxon King Alfred the Great (848–899).

Augustine's *Confessions* is one of history's earliest autobiographies. Consisting of thirteen books written in Latin between 397 and 400, it's a sincere, personal record of his life and spiritual journey. Augustine confesses his sins, past mistaken beliefs, and temptations, while also offering praise and prayers to God.

Written around 413–426, *The City of God* is Augustine's response to those who claimed that the Christian emperors' abolition of pagan worship led to the sacking of Rome by the Visigoths in 410. He maintained that Rome's fall was the result of internal moral decay, and Christianity saved it from complete destruction. He outlined two societies or *cities*—the City of God, consisting of God's faithful elect and founded on love of God, and the City of Man, consisting of the unbelieving damned and founded on love of self.

Meditations is a collection of early church prayers and devotions, along with teachings designed for priests and monks. It is believed that these were written toward the end of Augustine's life. The book was translated from Latin by George Stanhope for Princess Anne of Denmark in 1701.

Great are You, Lord, and greatly to be praised. Great is Your power, and Your wisdom is infinite. (See Psalm 145:3; 147:5.) And man wants to praise You; man, but a particle of Your creation; man, who bears his mortality, the witness of his sin, the witness that You *"resisteth the proud"* (James 4:6; 1 Peter 5:5). ... You awaken us to delight in Your praise, for You made us for Yourself, and our hearts are restless until they rest in You.

It is good to have the heart lifted up, yet not to one's self, for this is proud, but to the Lord, for this is obedient, and can be the act only of the humble. There is, therefore, something in humility that, strangely enough, exalts the heart, and something in pride that debases it. This seems, indeed, to be contradictory, that loftiness should debase and lowliness exalt.

Pious humility enables us to submit

to what is above us;

and nothing is more exalted

above us than God;

and therefore humility,

by making us subject to God,

exalts us.

I know, O Lord, and do with all humility acknowledge myself an object altogether unworthy of Your love; but I am sure You are an object altogether worthy of mine. I am not good enough to serve You, but You have a right to the best service I can pay. Impart to me some of that excellence, and it will supply my own lack of worth.

Help me to cease from sin according to Your will, that I may be capable of doing Your service according to my duty. Enable me to guard and govern myself, to begin and finish my course in such a way that when the race of life is run, I may sleep in peace and rest in You. Be with me to the end, that my sleep may be rest indeed, my rest perfect security, and that security a blessed eternity. Amen.

Faithfully interrogate your own souls, whether you have not been unduly puffed up by your integrity, continence, and chastity; and whether you have not been so desirous of the human praise that is accorded to these virtues that you have envied some who possessed them. I, for my part, do not know your hearts, and therefore I make no accusation; I do not even hear what your hearts answer when you question them. And yet, if they answer that it is as I have supposed it might be, do not marvel that you have lost that by which you can win men's praise and retain that which cannot be exhibited to men.

If you did not consent to sin,

it was because God added His aid to His grace

that it might not be lost, and because shame before men succeeded

to human glory that it might not be loved.

I know nothing better than that you should pray. Make your wish known to God, that you may through such salvation obtain what you wish. Write the prayer so you will be fitter for your task. And pray sincerely in few words and with full understanding.

Avarice is not a fault inherent in gold, but in the man who inordinately loves gold to the detriment of justice, which ought to be held in incomparably higher regard than gold. Luxury is not the fault of lovely and charming objects, but of the heart that inordinately loves sensual pleasures to the neglect of temperance, which attaches us to objects more lovely in their spirituality and more delectable by their incorruptibility. Nor yet is boasting the fault of human praise, but of the soul that is inordinately fond of the applause of men and that makes light of the voice of conscience. Pride, too, is not the fault of him who delegates power, nor of power itself, but of the soul that is inordinately enamored of its own power and despises the more just dominion of a higher authority.

He who inordinately loves the
good that any nature possesses,
even though he obtain it,
himself becomes evil in the
good and wretched because
deprived of a greater good.

Men are separated from God only by sins

from which we are in this life cleansed

not by our own virtue but by the divine compassion;

through His indulgence, not through our own power.

Those who want to obtain joy from external things soon become vain and waste themselves on things that are seen and temporal, and in their famished thoughts they lick their own shadows. If they were only worn out with their famine and would ask, "*Who will show us any good?*" (Psalm 4:6). And we would say, and they would hear, "*The light of thy countenance* [is sealed] *upon us*" (Psalm 4:6). We are not that light "*which lighteth every man*" (John 1:9), but we are enlightened by You, that having been darkness at one time, we may be light in You. (See Ephesians 5:8.)

Ignorance, and foolishness itself, is cloaked under the name of simplicity and harmlessness because nothing is found more single than You. And what is less injurious, since what injures the sinner are his own works? Sloth would gladly be at rest, but what more secure rest can be found besides in the Lord? Luxury aims at being called plenty and abundance, but You are the fullness and never-failing plenteousness of incorruptible pleasures.

Wastefulness presents a shadow of generosity, but You are the most overflowing giver of all good. Covetousness would possess many things, and You possess all things. Envy fights for excellency; what is more excellent than You? Anger seeks revenge; who revenges more justly than You?

Fear startles at unaccustomed and sudden things that endanger beloved things and takes forethought for their safety. But to You, what is unaccustomed or sudden, or who separates from You what You love? (See Romans 8:39.)

The freer you are from the things of this world,

the more clearly you shall understand

about the wisdom you desire.

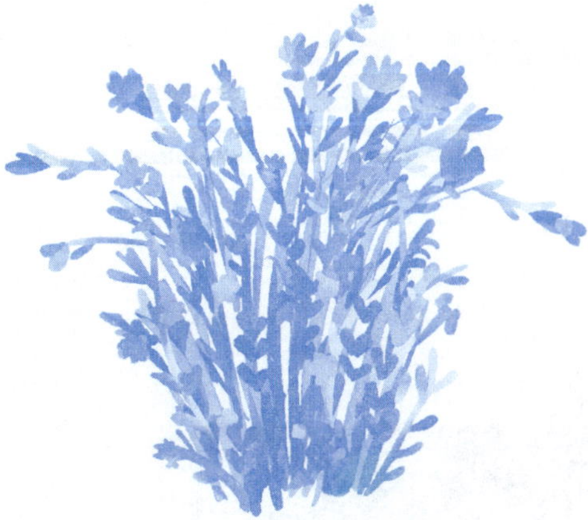

You are most high and are not changed (see Malachi 3:6), neither does today come to a close in You. Yet in You does it come to a close because all such things also are in You. For they had no way to pass away unless You upheld them. And since *"thy years shall have no end"* (Psalm 102:27), Your years are one today.

What are You then, my God? What but the Lord God? *"For who is God save the Lord?"* (Psalm 18:31). Or who is God save our God? Most high, most good, most potent, most omnipotent; most merciful, yet most just; most hidden, yet most present; most beautiful, yet most strong; stable, yet incomprehensible; unchangeable, yet all-changing; never new, never old; all-renewing and bringing age upon the proud, and they did not know it; ever working, ever at rest; still gathering, yet nothing lacking; supporting, filling, and overspreading; creating, nourishing, and maturing; seeking, yet having all things.

You love, without passion; are jealous, without anxiety; repent, yet grieve not; are angry, yet serene; change Your words, Your purpose unchanged; receive again what You find, yet never lost; never in need, yet rejoicing in gains; never covetous, yet exacting interest.

You receive over and above so that You may owe,

and who has anything that is not Yours? You pay debts,

owing nothing; remit debts, losing nothing.

And what have I now said, my God, my life, my holy joy?

Or what does any man say when he speaks of You?

Yet woe to him who does not speak,

since even the most eloquent are mute.

Since it is fit that the joyfulness of our hope should utter itself, and so show forth God's praise, and since it was from the profoundest sentiment of ardent and holy love that the psalmist cried, "O Lord, I have loved the beauty of Your house" (see Psalm 26:8), we may, with God's help, speak of the gifts He lavishes on men, good and bad alike, in this most wretched life and may do our best to conjecture the great glory of that state which we cannot worthily speak of, because we have not yet experienced it.

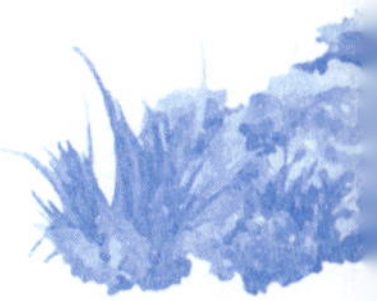

Let my soul praise You so that it may love You, and let it confess Your own mercies to You so that it may praise You. Your whole creation does not cease, nor is it silent in Your praises. Neither does the spirit of man cease Your praises through words directed to You. Creation, animate or inanimate, also praises You through the language of those who meditate on it, who look to those things You have created, and who move on from them to You who made them wonderfully, so that out of our weariness our souls may arise toward You. In these things there is refreshment and true strength.

You serve all the creatures that You did create; to You is every good soul subject; at Your command, the heavens turn and all the stars hold their courses; at Your order, the sun brings the bright day, and the moon light by night; You govern and wield all this world, so that all creatures change even as day and night.

You rule and fix the year by the alternations of the four seasons—spring, and summer, autumn, and winter—each of which alternates and varies with the other, so that each of them is again exactly what and where it formerly was; and so all the stars change and vary in the same manner.

How can I tell of the rest of creation, with all its beauty and utility, which the divine goodness has given to man to please his eye and serve his purposes, condemned though he is, and hurled into these labors and miseries?

Shall I speak of the manifold and various loveliness of sky, and earth, and sea; of the plentiful supply and wonderful qualities of the light; of sun, moon, and stars; of the shade of trees; of the colors and perfume of flowers; of the multitude of birds, all differing in plumage and in song; of the variety of animals, of which the smallest in size are often the most wonderful—the works of ants and bees astonishing us more than the huge bodies of whales?

Shall I speak of the sea, which itself is so grand a spectacle, when it arrays itself as it were in vestures of various colors, now running through every shade of green, and again becoming purple or blue? Is it not delightful to look at it in storm, and experience the soothing complacency it inspires, by suggesting that we ourselves are not tossed and shipwrecked?

What shall I say of the numberless kinds of food to alleviate hunger, and the variety of seasonings to stimulate appetite that are scattered everywhere by nature, and for which we are not indebted to the art of cookery? How many natural appliances are there for preserving and restoring health!

How grateful is the alternation of day and night! How pleasant the breezes that cool the air! How abundant the supply of clothing furnished us by trees and animals! Who can enumerate all the blessings we enjoy? If I were to attempt to detail and unfold only these few I have indicated, such an enumeration would fill a volume. And all these are but the solace of the wretched and condemned, not the rewards of the blessed. What then shall these rewards be, if such be the blessings of a condemned state?

Lord, You have made
all things perfect,
and nothing imperfect;
to You,
no creature is untoward;
though anything will,
it cannot be so.

There are many things, such as fire, frost, wild beasts, and so forth, which do not suit but injure this thin-blooded and frail mortality of our flesh, which is at present under just punishment. We do not consider how admirable these things are in their own places, how excellent in their own natures, how beautifully adjusted to the rest of creation, and how much grace they contribute to the universe by their own contributions.

How serviceable they are even to ourselves, if we use them with a knowledge of their fit adaptations—so that even poisons, which are destructive when used injudiciously, become wholesome and medicinal when used in conformity with their qualities and design; just as, on the other hand, those things that give us pleasure, such as food, drink, and the light of the sun, are found to be hurtful when immoderately or unseasonably used.

And thus divine providence admonishes us to not foolishly blame things, but to investigate their utility with care; and, where our mental capacity or infirmity is at fault, to believe that there is a utility, though hidden, as we have experienced that there were other things we all but failed to discover. This concealment of the use of things is itself either an exercise of our humility or a levelling of our pride; for no nature at all is evil, and this is a name for nothing but the want of good.

From earthly things
to heavenly things, from the
visible to the invisible, there
are some better than others;
and for this purpose are they
unequal, in order that they
might all exist.

God is such a great worker in great things that He is not less so in little things—for these little things are to be measured not by their own greatness, which does not exist, but by the wisdom of their Designer.

He alone, by that energy with which He works, causes the seed to develop and to evolve from certain secret and invisible folds into the visible forms of beauty we see. He alone, coupling and connecting in some wonderful fashion the spiritual and corporeal natures, the one to command, the other to obey, makes a living being.

This work of His is so great and wonderful that not only man, who is a rational animal, and consequently more excellent than all other animals of the earth, but even the most diminutive insect, cannot be considered attentively without astonishment and without praising the Creator.

To You I call, whom everything that can love loves, both those who know what they love, and those who do know what they love. You who have shaped all creatures very good, without any evil, I call to You, O Lord, because You are the Father of truth and wisdom, of the true and highest life, and of the highest blessedness, and of the highest good, and of the highest brightness, and of the intelligible light.

Not even lions or dragons

have ever waged with their

kind such wars as men

have waged with one another.

But God foresaw also that by His grace a people would be called to adoption, and that they, being justified by the remission of their sins, would be united by the Holy Spirit to the holy angels in eternal peace, the last enemy, death, being destroyed; and He knew that this people would derive profit from the consideration that God had caused all men to be derived from one, for the sake of showing how highly He prizes unity in a multitude.

What tigress does not gently purr over her cubs and lay aside her ferocity to fondle them? What kite, solitary as he is when circling over his prey, does not seek a mate, build a nest, hatch the eggs, bring up the young birds, and maintain with the mother of his family as peaceful a domestic alliance as he can? How much more powerfully do the laws of man's nature move him to hold fellowship and maintain peace with all men.

Peace is a good so great that even in this earthly and mortal life there is no word we hear with such pleasure, nothing we desire with such zest or find to be more thoroughly gratifying.

What else was meant by His word through the prophet, "I will be your God, and you shall be My people" (see Leviticus 26:12) than, I shall be their satisfaction, I shall be all that men honorably desire—life, and health, and nourishment, and plenty, and glory, and honor, and peace, and all good things?

He shall be the end of our desires who shall

be seen without end, loved without cloy,

praised without weariness.

I call on You, O Lord, who made all that could not else have sprung into being, nor without You could even abide. I call to You, O Lord, who leave none of Your creatures to become naught. To You I call, who has made all creatures beautiful without any original substance. To You I call, who never wrought any evil, but rather every good work. To You I call, who teaches a few wise men that evil is naught.

You, Lord, who formed me, know the work of Your own hands, and yet, because I am Your creature, I have been bold to ask many and great mercies, though less than and altogether unworthy of the least of all Your mercies. (See Genesis 32:10.)

I acknowledge, O my God, with shame and sorrow,

that not only the gifts and graces I have been imploring

all this while are in no degree my due;

but that many and grievous sufferings and judgments are

what I have justly deserved at Your hands.

When my soul feels itself sinking under the weight of this melancholy reflection, the publicans, harlots, and sinners (see Matthew 21:31), those wandering and lost sheep (see Luke 15:4), which the good Shepherd sought so carefully, drew back from the very brink of the hellish precipice so seasonably, brought home upon His shoulders so joyfully, and laid in His bosom so affectionately; these raise my drooping spirits and give new life to my hopes.

For You, my God, have made all things by Your power and are wonderful in all Your doings; yet You are most wonderful, and exceedingly glorious in Your works of pity and love. In this sense too is that most true, which You speak of Yourself by the mouth of Your servants. *"The Lord is good to all: and his tender mercies are over all his works"* (Psalm 145:9). And what was said of one particular person, we may most truly apply to Your people in general, My mercy will I not take from him. (See Psalm 89:28.)

For You abhor, despise,

forsake no man;

but such only as,

lost to all sense of their

own duty and happiness,

do first despise and forsake You.

You give good things liberally,

upon the request of those wretches who

have provoked You to anger.

O my God, the horn of my salvation and my refuge,

I am sadly sensible that I am one of those miserable wretches;

I have provoked Your wrath and done evil in Your sight;

and yet You stay Your hand.

I have sinned, You have suffered: I have offended, and still You bear with me. If I repent, You spare me; if I return, You receive me with open arms; nay, even while I delay, You wait patiently for my coming back to You.

You call me to You, when I go astray; You invite me while I am deaf to Your gracious calls; You stay till I shake off my wicked sloth; and, when Your prodigal child at last reflects on himself, You meet and embrace him most gladly.

You instruct my ignorance, comfort my sorrows,

keep me from falling, raise me up when I have fallen,

give when I ask, are found when I seek You,

and open the door when I knock. (See Matthew 7:7.)

Thus, O God of my salvation, I have nothing to offer in my own excuse; no plea to make when You charge me with folly. There is no refuge for me except in Your goodness and protection; no place to hide me from Your all-seeing eye.

You have shown me the right way;

You have taught me how

I ought to walk in it;

You have threatened the

torments of hell to frighten me

from wickedness;

and promised the joys of heaven

to encourage my obedience.

And now, O Father of mercies and God

of all comfort, I beseech You

to perfect these gracious designs

upon Your servant;

possess me thoroughly with

Your fear, that I may not dare

to incur Your threats;

and support me with the joy

of Your salvation,

that I may be filled with Your love,

and cheerfully run the race

that leads to Your gracious promises.

You, O Lord, are my strength,
my God, my refuge and only deliverer:
O be You pleased to inspire my soul
with proper thoughts of You:
teach my tongue fit words
to call upon You acceptably;
and enable my hands,
and every member,
to do the thing that pleases You.

Suffer me not, O Strength of my soul's health, suffer me not, I beg, to be one of those weak Christians, who "*for a while believe, and in time of temptation fall away*" (Luke 8:13). But cover my head in the day of battle; for You are my hope in the day of trouble and my safety in the time of danger. (See Psalm 140:7; 46:1.)

Thus do I come to You, *"my light and my salvation"* (Psalm 27:1), imploring the blessings of which I stand in need and declaring the miseries of which I am afraid. But in the midst of this address, I feel a check from within; my conscience stings, and my heart misgives me; love bids me hope, but sense of sin bids me fear; and dread of Your displeasure damps that zeal with which my heart approaches You. When I reflect on my own doings, I cannot but despond; when I look up to Your goodness, I am full of hope.

The kindness of my God invites and pushes me forward;

the wickedness of my own heart dismays and pulls me back.

And all my faults appear in such ghastly shapes before my eyes,

as almost hinder a holy confidence,

but quite beat down the boldness of presumption.

Do the heaven and earth contain You since You fill them? Or do You fill them and yet overflow since they do not contain You? And where, when the heaven and the earth are filled, do You pour forth the remainder of Yourself? Or do You have no need that anything should contain You, who contain all things, since what You fill, You fill by containing it? For the vessels that You fill do not uphold You, since though they were broken, You were not poured out. And when You are poured out on us, You are not cast down, but You uplift us; You are not dissipated, but You gather us.

O God most high, three Persons, but one essence, the same majesty and power, Lord God Almighty! The least of all Your servants and weakest member of Your mystical body, the church, desires to ascribe to You all honor and praise, the utmost that the little knowledge and power with which You have been pleased to endue him is capable of.

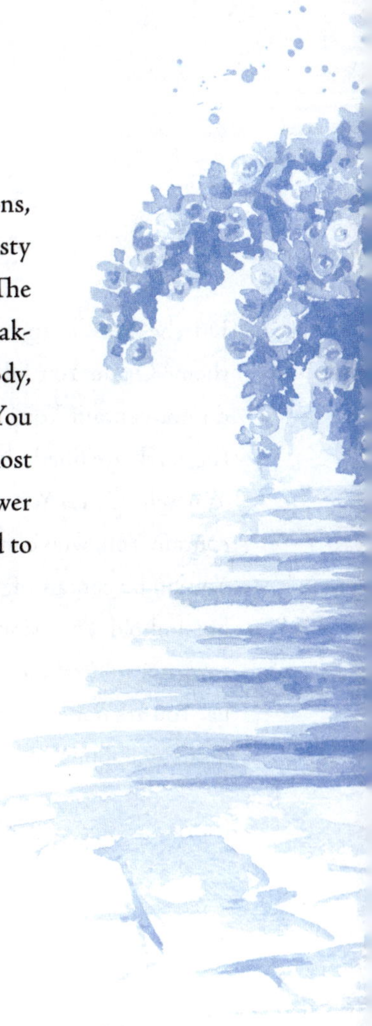

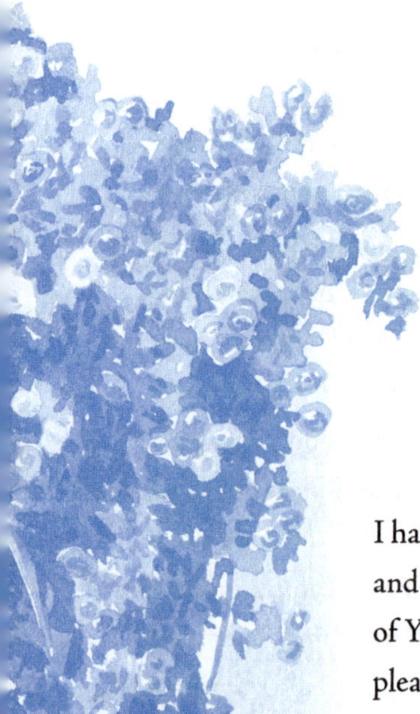

I have no present but myself to make, and that which is not in itself worthy of Your acceptance, I beg You will be pleased to look upon, not according to its own value, but according to Your own rich mercy and that sincerity and faith unfeigned, with which I do most joyfully consecrate to Your service.

I believe in, and heartily pray to You, great King of heaven and earth; I acknowledge Father, Son, and Holy Spirit; three Persons, but one essence; the true, the Almighty God, of one uncompounded, incorporeal, invisible, uncircumscribed being; in whom there is nothing higher or lower, greater or less, but perfect and equal all: great without quantity, good without quality, eternal without time, life without death, strength without weakness, truth without falsehood, omnipresent without space, filling all things and places without extension, passing everywhere without motion, abiding everywhere without confinement, communicating to all Your creatures without diminishing Your own fullness, governing all things without labor; without beginning, and yet giving beginning to all; making all things mutable, and yet unchangeable Yourself; infinite in greatness, unbounded in power, of goodness indefectible, of wisdom incomprehensible, wonderful in Your counsels, just in Your judgments, unsearchable in Your thoughts, true in all Your words, holy in all Your works, abundant in mercies, longsuffering toward sinners, compassionate to all who repent; always the same, without mixture or defilement, allay or accidents; eternal, immortal, unchangeable.

Your will alters not, Your justice is not biased,

Your mind is not disturbed with griefs, or pleasures,

or passions: with You nothing is forgotten,

nothing that was once lost called to remembrance again;

but all things past or future are ever present to

Your capacious mind: whose duration neither begun in time,

nor increases by length of time, nor shall it ever end,

but You live before, and in, and after all ages.

Your glory is eternal, Your power supreme,

Your kingdom everlasting, and world without end. Amen.

You are neither enlarged by
any addition of space,
nor changed by any revolution of time.
You inhabit the light,
which no man can approach;
indivisible, because strictly
and simply One, having no parts,
You fill all things with
the whole of Yourself.

Finite minds cannot distinctly conceive,
nor artful expressions declare,
nor whole volumes and libraries
explain the depths and intricacies
of this mystery.
For what can describe the
greatness that is above all quantity,
and the transcendent goodness
that is above all quality?

This is perfect goodness indeed;

and therefore none is truly good except You alone,

with whom to intend is to finish and

to will is to be able to perform.

You made all things out of nothing, merely because it was Your good pleasure so to do. You possess all things, not because You need any: You govern all without care or toil, and nothing in heaven above, or in earth, no not in hell beneath, has power to countermand, or in any degree to disturb Your regular management, or break the beauteous order of Your universe.

You cannot repent of anything

You have done because

Your wisdom always does the best;

nor can You be disordered with

any tumultuous passions,

for these are the tempests

and commotions of weak minds.

You never lie, because You are eternal truth: we are created by Your bounty alone; by Your justice we are punished for our offenses; and by Your clemency we are delivered from vengeance and destruction.

You alone have self-existence and

never change from what You are:

Hence is Your name Jehovah,

the self-existent one,

denoting that You are always the same,

and Your years shall not fail. (See Psalm 102:27.)

You are the One, the true God, without body, parts, or passions. No part of Your substance is capable of change or corruption, compounded or made. This makes it evident that no bodily eye can discern You, and that no mortal can see You in Your proper essence: for this reason it is also plain that from the same cause, which enables angels to be behold You now, we also after this life shall be enabled to behold You.

If man has been so created as to attain, through that which is most excellent in him, to that which excels all things—that is, to the one true and absolutely good God, without whom no nature exists, no doctrine instructs, no exercise profits—let Him be sought in whom all things are secure to us, let Him be discovered in whom all truth becomes certain to us, let Him be loved in whom all becomes right to us.

Even though the arrogant may mock me,

those who have not been,

for the good of their souls,

stricken and cast down by You,

my God, I will still confess to You

my own shame in Your praise.

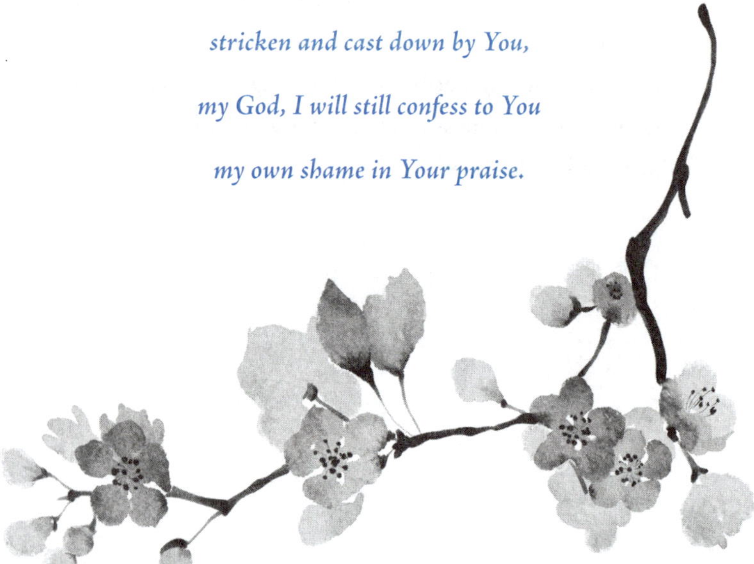

My soul is distracted with different passions when I appear before the Divine Majesty. Alas! How could it be otherwise? For with what face can man, who has deserved nothing but hatred and indignation, entreat a favor? What rashness is it to ask for glory, when punishment only is his due?

A naughty child provokes

a most affectionate father,

and is it not yet a greater

provocation to

assume to himself the

claim of inheriting,

till he has first retracted

his undutiful behavior?

This, O my Father, I confess with grief to be my own case, I ask life, and have deserved death; I have been disloyal to my King, and yet have the confidence to fly to Him for protection; I have despised my Judge, and armed His angry justice against my guilty self, and yet this very Judge I go to for support. I have stopped my ears against the commands of a Father, and yet I take upon myself to depend on Him for His paternal affection and care.

My feet, alas! are swift to ruin,

but slow in the way that leads to life and safety.

I.run after sickness, and wounds, and death,

and take no care to shun the darts that made those wounds,

even when I have felt the smart and am healed of the sore.

I did not prevent those dangers that might have been avoided,

and I am at last awakened into a sense of them when they have

brought me to the very gates of the grave.

How often I have offended, it is not in my power to remember: but this I own with a heavy heart, that, in general, I have taught men how to sin, and made them wise and skillful in wickedness, those who lived before in happy ignorance of it. I have persuaded them who were averse, forced them who resisted me, and readily complied and taken part with those whose inclinations were to do amiss. I have laid snares for those who walked securely; betrayed those into the pit, who desired to be informed in the right way; and, that I might dare to be guilty of those things, I have dared to forget and drive out of my mind those good principles, and great obligations of gratitude to so good a God, which should have restrained me from them.

But how faulty whatsoever

my own memory may be,

yet I have to deal with a

just and terrible Judge:

one who seals up my iniquities in

a bag and spies out all my ways.

God gave freedom to men's souls,

that they might do either good or evil,

whichever they would choose;

and promised good for a reward

to those who do good,

and evil to those who do evil.

The grace of God could not have been more graciously commended to us than this, that the only Son of God, remaining unchangeable in Himself, should assume humanity and should give us the hope of His love, by means of the mediation of a human nature, through which we, from the condition of men, might come to Him who was so far off—the immortal from the mortal; the unchangeable from the changeable; the just from the unjust; the blessed from the wretched. As He had given us a natural instinct to desire blessedness and immortality, He Himself continuing to be blessed, but assuming mortality, by enduring what we fear, taught us to despise it, that what we long for He might bestow upon us.

All wisdom without You is no better than folly, and to know You alone is the sum and perfection of knowledge. Inform me, therefore, O Divine Wisdom, and make me understand Your statutes. For I am fully persuaded, that he, and he alone, is blessed whom You nurture and teach in Your law. (See Psalm 94:12.)

My desire is to call upon You, and to do it in truth: but what can calling upon truth itself in truth mean, except applying to the Father by the Son? Therefore, holy Father, Your Word is truth, and the beginning of all Your Word in the gospel has told us, *"In the beginning was the Word"* (John 1:1).

What can be more delightful than to address Him that begot, in the name of His only begotten? Than to move the Father to tenderness by the mention of His own dear Son? Than to appease the wrath of a King, by interposing the darling of the family, the heir of all His dominions?

A king's anger cools instantly,

if the offenders are such favorites of the prince

as to make use of his name and interest;

and servants find it no hard matter to come off

without punishment if the children employ their

pretty endearments in their behalf.

Since then these methods are so successful below,

why should they not have the same good effect above?

I will beg the almighty Father, for the sake of His almighty Son, *"Bring my soul out of prison, that I may praise* [His] *name"* (Psalm 142:7). Loose me, Lord, from the bands of my sins, for the sake of Your only, Your co-eternal Son; and by the intercession of that dear, that divine image and brightness of Your glory, now sitting at Your right hand, be reconciled to a poor sinful wretch; and, instead of that death my wickedness deservedly threatens me with, raise and restore me to a life of hope and blessedness.

This therefore is my Mediator with You, heavenly Father; this my perfect High Priest, who does not need to be sanctified with other blood, but has made atonement, and stands before You, pure and bright, in virtue of His own blood, with which He was washed for our sakes. This is that holy and unblemished sacrifice, acceptable and perfect, offered for a sweet-smelling savor unto God. This is that Lamb without spot, who was mute before His shearers; and though reviled, and buffeted, and spit upon, yet He did not open His mouth. (See Isaiah 53:7.) This is that righteous Person, who did not sin, but condescended to bear our sins and heal our putrefied sores by His own stripes.

What have You done, O charming innocence, to bring You as a criminal before Your enemies' bar? Or how have You deserved to be treated with such rude and insolent, such unrelenting and triumphant barbarity? What passage of Your whole life could they fix an accusation upon, what crime allege to countenance so rigorous a sentence? If none, as none they could, then where did Your shameful bitter death come from, or how did You come to be condemned as a vile miscreant?

It was I, alas! it was wretched I,

who gave You all those pains:

it was I who deserved the death that You endured;

and my offenses gave those scourges,

those nails, that spear,

the power of staying and wounding,

and killing You.

O wonderful process! Mystery of justice! That the wicked should offend, and the righteous be punished for it! That the guilt and the condemnation should thus be separated! That the servant should contract a debt, and the Lord, to whom it was due, make satisfaction! That man should provoke the divine vengeance, and God should feel the smart of it! How low, O Son of God, did Your humility stoop! How fervent was Your love! How boundless Your compassion!

I have done wickedly,

and You are called to account for it:

I armed an angry justice against myself,

and it is discharged upon Your head:

mine is the crime,

and Yours the torture:

I have been proud, and You are humbled;

I am puffed up,

and You have emptied Yourself:

I have been rebellious,

and Your obedience has atoned for it.

I have been intemperate,

and You have hungered and thirsted for it:

my ungoverned appetite sinned in the forbidden,

and Your immense love submitted to hang on the accursed tree:

I eat the fruit, and You feel the pains:

I wallow in pleasures, and You are torn with nails:

the honey in my mouth is turned to gall

in Your stomach.

The tempting Eve rejoices with me,

the sorrowful Mary suffers and laments with You.

Thus is my wickedness and want of love to God,

thus is Your righteousness and inexpressible love

to man manifested in this marvelous dispensation.

How should a poor creature be capable of any recompense suitable to the mercy of an almighty Creator? And yet, my dearest Savior, so wonderfully is this matter ordered that even man, even I, weak and worthless though I be, may find something that You are pleased to accept in return; if by Your grace my soul be broken and humbled, and I crucify this flesh with its *"affections and lusts"* (Galatians 5:24).

By gaining a conquest upon the inward man, You enable me to win the crown by my outward man; and, by triumphing over the flesh in spiritual trials, that very flesh has the courage to submit gladly for Your sake to bodily persecutions and death. This is the utmost my condition will admit; and this, though but little in itself, yet when proceeding from the same principle of holy love, You are graciously pleased to accept, as the utmost poor mortals can do in acknowledgment of their great Maker.

I beseech You, therefore, by

"thy tender mercies [*which*] have been ever of old" (*Psalm 25:6*),

pour such balm into my wounds as

may dispel the venom of my diseases,

and restore me to spiritual health and soundness.

Let me drink of Your heavenly sweetness, and be so ravished with the taste, as ever after to dislike the sensual delights of the world, to despise its pleasures, and cheerfully encounter the afflictions of this present life; and so to fix my heart on true noble joys, as always to disdain the empty and transitory shadows, which flesh and blood is so foolishly fond of, and so fearful of parting with.

Let me hate most irreconcilably whatever displeases You; and what You love let me most eagerly desire and incessantly pursue: let me feel no satisfaction in any joys without You; nor any reluctancy in the greatest sufferings for You.

Let the mention of Your name
be always a refreshment,
and the remembrance of
Your goodness an inexhaustible
spring of comfort to my soul.

Let tears be my food day and night, so I may attain to Your righteousness; and *"the law of thy mouth"* be always dearer to me *"than thousands of gold and silver"* (Psalm 119:72).

Let me aim at nothing so much as to do You service; nor detest and avoid anything in comparison of sinning against You. And, for what I have unhappily done of that kind already, I entreat You, my only refuge and hope, to pardon for Your own mercy's sake.

Let my ears be ever open to the voice of Your law, and do not allow my heart to incline *"to any evil thing"* (Psalm 141:4), so that I never comply with those who practice wickedness, nor take shelter in trifling pretenses to excuse or indulge myself in doing what I should not.

You, Lord, are good and merciful,

and Your right hand has respected the depth of my death and,

from the bottom of my heart,

has emptied that abyss of corruption.

And Your whole gift to me was not to will what I willed,

and to will what You willed.

Now my soul was free from the biting cares of seeking and getting, weltering in filth, and scratching off the itch of lust. And my infant tongue spoke freely to You, my brightness and my riches and my health, Lord my God.

Too late I loved You,

Beauty of Ancient Days,

yet ever new!

Too late I loved You!

Behold, You were within me,

and I was outside of You.

There I searched for You,

I who was deformed,

plunging amid those beautiful things

You had made.

You called and shouted and burst my deafness. You flashed, shone, and scattered my blindness. You breathed aromas, and I drew in breath, and now I pant for You. I tasted You, and now I hunger and thirst. You touched me, and I burned for Your peace.

My hope, my Christ, my God, Savior and lover of men, You light and way, You life and health, You glory and grace of all who love and serve You! Look down from the throne of Your majesty, and in the midst of bliss remember the injuries and sufferings, the scourges, and the cross, the wounds and death that You endured—and think with favor on Your suppliant, for whose sake You were pleased to endure and do so much.

You are my living and true God; my holy Father, my gentle and kind Master, my great King, my good Shepherd, my only Teacher, my most ready and effectual Helper, my dearest and most beautiful Spouse, my true and living Bread, my everlasting High Priest, my Guide to my own country, my true Light, my right Way, my best Wisdom, my holy delight, my unspotted purity, my reconciliation and peace, my sure defense; my most desirable portion; my eternal health; my unbounded mercy; my invincible patience; my unblemished sacrifice; my perfect redemption; my assured hope; my universal charity; my resurrection from the dead; my everlasting life; my joy and beatific vision forever.

Give me Yourself,

O God, give me Your love in return,

for that I love You, You know;

and if it be too little,

I desire to love You more ardently.

I cannot make such exact reckoning of my love, as to know how much I fall short of the affection that I ought to have, that so my every action and desire might carry me to Your embraces, fly to Your arms, and never cease the pursuit of my Lord, till I am hidden in the secret place of Your presence. Though I cannot take a precise measure of my defects, and how much better I ought to be, yet this I know and from my own experience can declare, that all without, nay, all besides You, avails me nothing.

Open Your door to me, and teach me how to come in. I have nothing to bring You but good will, for I myself have nothing else, nor do I know anything better than to love the heavenly and the spiritual above the earthly; and this I do, good Father, since I know nothing better than that.

You most ancient and most wise Father, I commit to You my body, that You may keep it whole. Yet I do not know what I ask—whether I am asking a thing useful or useless to me; nor do I know how long You will keep my body whole. Therefore I commit and commend it to You. I pray that You always teach me, while I am in this body and this world, and help me always. Teach me and free me from error.

And now, O Holy Spirit, love of God, who proceeds from the Almighty Father and His most blessed Son, powerful Advocate, and sweetest Comforter, infuse Your grace, and descend plentifully into my heart; enlighten the dark corners of this neglected dwelling, and scatter there Your cheerful beams! Dwell in the soul that longs to be Your temple; water the barren soil, overrun with weeds and briars, and lost for lack of cultivating, and make it fruitful with Your dew from heaven.

I believe, O Holy Spirit, that in whomsoever You dwell, the Father and the Son do likewise come, and inhabit that person. And, oh! happy is the one who is honored with so glorious, so divine a guest, in whose company the Father and the Son always come and take up their abode! O that it may please You to come to me, You kindest comforter of mourning souls, You mighty defense in distresses, and ready help in time of need.

Breathe in me, O Holy Spirit,

That my thoughts may all be holy.

Act in me, O Holy Spirit,

That my work, too, may be holy.

Draw my heart, O Holy Spirit,

That I love but what is holy.

Strengthen me, O Holy Spirit,

To defend all that is holy.

Guard me, then, O Holy Spirit,

That I always may be holy.

O brightness of Your Father's glory, who from Your throne far above the cherubim sees all the secrets of the great deep! You true, enlivening, unexhausted light, which angels long to be illuminated with, and spend glad ages in beholding! spring forth into my soul, and scatter the thick darkness there, that the brightness of Your love may shine and shed itself through every corner of my benighted heart.

O sweetest, kindest, dearest Jesus! Pour into me, I beg You, the abundance of Your love, that there may be no remains of earthly or sensual desires or thoughts in my breast, but You and Your love may reign unrivaled there and possess my heart entirely. Write Your name in my mind so that You and Your commands may be ever before my eyes. Kindle in my soul that holy fire which You have sent into the world, that it may melt away my dross and qualify me for offering to You the daily sacrifice of a broken and contrite spirit.

We tend toward Him by love,

that we may rest in Him,

and find our blessedness by attaining that end.

For our good,

about which philosophers have so keenly contended,

is nothing else than to be united to God.

He departed from our eyes so that we might return into our hearts and find Him there. He departed, and behold, He is here. He was not with us very long, yet He did not leave us. For He departed from here, from where He never really parted because *"the world was made by him"* (John 1:10).